OS X
Troubleshooting

Yosemite Edition

DIANE YEE

Questing Vole Press

OS X Troubleshooting, Yosemite Edition
by Diane Yee

Editor: Bill Gregory
Proofreader: Pat Kissell
Compositor: Birgitte Lund
Cover: Questing Vole Press

Contents

CHAPTER 1

Getting Started

Troubleshooting is the systematic, iterative process of identifying and fixing problems, in which you:

1 Analyze plausible causes based on symptoms

2 Identify potential solutions

3 Apply a fix

4 Evaluate the results

5 Return to step 1 if the fix fails

OS X has built-in tools that help you identify and resolve various system-related problems, including startup issues, networking issues, and general issues such as slowness and permissions problems. This book shows you how to troubleshoot the following types of problems:

- **Hardware problems.** Your Mac shuts down abruptly or won't boot, for example, possibly because of a bad drive or a faulty fan.

- **Software problems.** An application won't open, for example, or an error occurs every time that you try to save a document.

- **Environmental problems.** Your Ethernet connection works fine in the office but never at home, for example.

- **User errors.** The problem is not the hardware, software, or environment, but how you choose to do things.

Conventions Used in This Book

A shorthand instruction to navigate to a nested folder or to choose a command looks like this:

Choose > System Preferences > Dock > Position on Screen > Left.

Each name between the > symbols refers to an icon, folder, window, dialog box, menu, button, checkbox, option, link, or pane; just look on the screen for a matching label. The refers to the Apple menu, in the top-left corner of the desktop.

Keyboard shortcuts are given in the form "Shift+Command+N".

CHAPTER 2

Using Startup Commands

S tartup commands make a Mac or device perform a specific task while the system is starting (booting). OS X has several startup commands that can help you troubleshoot issues that occur before you log in.

Though startup problems can have any number of causes, they can often be solved with a simple startup command. In OS X, you issue a startup command by holding down a combination of keys while your Mac powers up. The following table lists OS X's common startup commands, some of which are covered in later chapters.

Tip: Startup commands typically address high-level problems, such as battery life, rather than narrow issues, such as problems with specific apps or documents. But if you're desperate or feel that a startup command might be relevant, then go ahead and use it—it's quick and harmless.

To invoke a startup command, hold down the key(s) listed in Table 2.1 when you turn on your Mac (press the power button ⏻). Unless otherwise specified, hold down the specified key(s) immediately after you hear the startup tone (while the screen is still black).

Table 2.1 OS X Startup Commands

Hold Down	To
Left Shift key, when you see the spinning progress indicator	Prevent automatic login.
Shift, after clicking the Log In button in the login window	Prevent login items and Finder windows from opening when you log in.
C	Start from a CD or DVD.
N	Start from the default NetBoot (network-based) disk image.
T	Start in target disk mode. For details, read the Apple support article "How to use and troubleshoot FireWire target disk mode" at *support.apple.com/ht1661*.
D	Use Apple Diagnostics or Apple Hardware Test.
Command+R	Use OS X Recovery tools. See Chapter 6.
Option	Select an OS X volume or network volume to start from.
Eject (⏏) or F12, or hold down the mouse or trackpad button	Eject any removable media, such as an optical disc.
Option+Command+P+R	Reset NVRAM (also called PRAM). See Chapter 4.
Command+V	Show detailed status messages in verbose mode. See Chapter 5.
Command+S	Start in single-user mode to troubleshoot your Mac's startup sequence by using only UNIX commands. Use this mode only if you're comfortable with UNIX.

Hold Down	To
Shift, immediately after you hear the startup tone	Start in safe mode. See Chapter 5.
Shift+Control+Option	Reset the SMC (System Management Controller). See Chapter 3.

Tip: To force-restart your Mac, press and hold the power button ⏻ for about 10 seconds until the Mac shuts down. After a moment, press the power button again to start your Mac. You will lose any unsaved work in any open applications when you force a shut down.

Resetting the SMC

The **SMC (System Management Controller)** is a device that's responsible for many of your Mac's lower-level functions, including:

- Responding to presses of the power button ⏻

- Responding to the display lid opening and closing on a portable Mac (MacBook Pro, MacBook Air, or MacBook)

- Battery management

- Thermal (internal temperature) management

- The SMS (Sudden Motion Sensor)

- Ambient light sensing

- Keyboard backlighting

- Status Indicator Light (SIL) management

- Battery status indicator lights

- Selecting an external (instead of internal) video source for some iMac displays

Symptoms

Table 3.1 lists symptoms associated with a poorly functioning SMC.

Table 3.1 Symptoms for SMC-Related Problems

Problem Area	Symptoms
Fans	▪ The Mac's fans run at high speed even though the computer isn't being used heavily and is ventilated properly.
Lights	▪ The keyboard backlight misbehaves (on Macs that have this feature).
	▪ The Status Indicator Light (SIL) misbehaves (on Macs that have an SIL).
	▪ Battery indicator lights misbehave (on portable Macs that use nonremovable batteries).
	▪ The display backlight responds incorrectly to changes in ambient light (on Macs that have this feature).
Power	▪ The Mac doesn't respond to the power button ⏻ when pressed.
	▪ A portable Mac doesn't respond properly when you close or open the lid.
	▪ The Mac sleeps or shuts down unexpectedly.
	▪ The battery doesn't charge properly.
	▪ The power adaptor LED indicates the wrong charging status.
System performance	▪ The Mac runs slowly even when CPU usage (page 40) is low.
	▪ Application icons in the dock continue to "bounce" long after the app is opened.
	▪ Applications work incorrectly or stop responding after being opened.

Problem Area	Symptoms
Video	■ A Mac switches into or out of target display mode External link unexpectedly, or fails to switch into or out of target display mode (for Macs that support this mode). For details, read the Apple support article "Target Display Mode: Frequently Asked Questions (FAQ)" at *support.apple.com/ht3924*.
Port illumination	■ The I/O ports don't illuminate when you move the Mac (for Mac Pros, late 2013 or newer).

Before Resetting the SMC

In some cases, resetting the SMC might be the only correct way to fix a problem related to the symptoms listed above. However, you should reset SMC only after you try all other standard troubleshooting methods. Try each of the following steps in order before you reset the SMC. Test the issue after completing each troubleshooting step to determine whether the problem is fixed.

1   Press Command+Option+Escape to force-quit any application that's not responding.

2   Put your Mac to sleep by choosing > Sleep, and then wake your Mac after it has gone to sleep.

3   Restart your Mac by choosing > Restart.

4   Shut down your Mac by choosing > Shut Down, and then turn on your Mac after it has shut down.

Tip: If your Mac doesn't respond to > Shut Down, then you can force it to shut down by pressing and holding the power button for about 10 seconds until the Mac shuts down. You will lose any unsaved work in any open applications when you force a shut down.

If you have a portable Mac (MacBook Pro, MacBook Air, or MacBook) that's experiencing a problem related to the power adapter or battery, then do the following additional steps:

▪   Unplug the power adapter from the Mac *and* the power socket for several seconds.

▪   Shut down the Mac (> Shut Down), physically remove and then re-insert the battery (if it's removable), and then turn on the Mac.

Resetting the SMC

If the problem still isn't resolved after following the troubleshooting steps above, then reset the SMC. This procedure varies by Mac model.

To reset the SMC on a MacBook Pro (early 2009 or newer), MacBook Air (any model), or MacBook (late 2009 or newer):

1   Shut down the Mac (🍎 > Shut Down).

2   Plug in the power adapter to a power source, connecting it to the Mac if it's not already connected.

3   On the built-in keyboard, press the (left side) Shift+Control+Option keys and the power button ⏻ at the same time for a few seconds (Figure 3.1).

4   Release all the keys and the power button at the same time.

5   Press the power button ⏻ to turn on the Mac.

Tip: The LED on the power adapter may change colors or turn off temporarily when you reset the SMC.

Shift   Control   Option

Figure 3.1 Keyboard shortcut to reset the SMC.

To reset the SMC on a Mac Pro, Intel-based iMac, Intel-based Mac mini, or Intel-based Xserve:

1 Shut down the Mac (> Shut Down).

2 Unplug the Mac's power cord.

3 Wait fifteen seconds.

4 Attach the Mac's power cord.

5 Wait five seconds, and then press the power button to turn on the Mac.

To reset the SMC on a MacBook Pro (pre-2009) or MacBook (pre-2010):

1 Shut down the Mac (> Shut Down).

2 Disconnect the power adapter from the Mac, if it's connected.

3 Remove the battery.

4 Press and hold the power button for 5 seconds.

5 Release the power button.

6 Reinstall the battery.

7 Reconnect the power adapter.

8 Press the power button to turn on the Mac.

Tip: Resetting the SMC doesn't reset, or otherwise change, the contents of NVRAM (Chapter 4).

Resetting NVRAM

A small amount of your Mac's memory, called **NVRAM (non-volatile random access memory)**, stores certain settings in a location that OS X can access quickly. The particular settings that are stored depend on your Mac model and the types of devices connected to it. These settings include your time zone, startup volume choice, speaker volume, and DVD region setting. "Non-volatile" means that the stored information remains in place even after you shut down or restart your Mac.

Tip: NVRAM is called **PRAM (parameter random access memory)** on older PowerPC Macs. Despite the difference in nomenclature, the two types of RAM both have a similar purpose.

Symptoms

Symptoms associated with corrupted NVRAM include:

- Wrong system date

- Flashing folder with a question mark

- Slow startup

- No sound

Tip: To list the settings stored in NVRAM, open the Terminal application, type `nvram -p`, and then press Return.

Resetting NVRAM

To reset NVRAM:

1   Shut down your Mac (**** > Shut Down).

2   Press and release the power button ⏻ and then immediately press and hold the Option+Command+P+R keys simultaneously (Figure 4.1).

You must press this key combination before the gray screen appears.

3   Continue holding the keys down until your Mac restarts and you hear the startup sound for the second time, and then release the keys.

4   After you log in, choose **** > System Preferences, and then reselect your usual startup disk, time zone, and sound volume. (Resetting NVRAM returns these settings to their default values.)

Tip: NVRAM doesn't store display and network settings, as it did in some older versions of OS X. If you're having problems with video or networking, resetting NVRAM probably won't help.

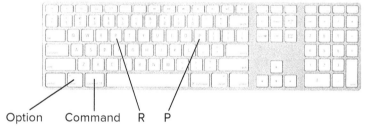

Option   Command   R   P

Figure 4.1 Keyboard shortcut to reset NVRAM.

CHAPTER 5

Starting in Safe Mode or Verbose Mode

Use safe mode and verbose mode to resolve or isolate problems caused by:

- Corrupt applications (freezes or crashes)
- Corrupt data
- Newly installed programs and extensions
- Damaged fonts
- Damaged preference settings
- Corrupt startup sequences (boot failures or freezes)

Starting in Safe Mode

Starting your Mac in **safe mode** (sometimes called **safe boot**) performs certain checks and prevents some software from loading or opening automatically. Safe mode:

- Verifies the startup disk, and attempts to repair any directory issues

- Loads only required kernel extensions

- Prevents login items and Finder windows from opening automatically

- Disables all user-installed (third-party) fonts

- Moves font caches (located in /Library/Caches/com.apple.ATS/*uid*/) to the Trash

To start in safe mode:

1 Shut down your Mac ( > Shut Down).

2 Press and release the power button ⏻.

3 Immediately after you hear the startup sound, press and hold the Shift key (Figure 5.1).

   Press the Shift key as soon as possible after startup, but not before the startup sound.

4 Release Shift when the Apple logo appears.

   A progress bar indicates that safe mode is performing a directory check (which slows the boot process).

Tip: When your Mac is in safe mode, the words "Safe Mode" appear in the upper-right corner of the login screen, and the Software section of System Information (Applications > Utilities > System Information) lists the Boot Mode as "Safe" instead of "Normal".

Shift

Figure 5.1 Keyboard shortcut to start in safe mode.

Safe mode disables or limits certain features:

- DVD Player won't work

- iMovie can't capture video

- Devices connected to audio in/out ports won't work

- Internal and external modems won't work

- Some USB, FireWire, and Thunderbolt devices may not be available

- Wi-fi networking might be limited or unavailable

- Hardware-accelerated graphics are disabled (no translucency, for example)

- Network file sharing is disabled (you can't mount Time Capsule drives, for example)

- Third-party extensions and fonts are disabled

With your Mac in safe mode, you can troubleshoot by systematically eliminating suspected culprits: uninstall a recently installed third-party application, remove a startup or login item, or repair permissions (Chapter 11), for example.

To exit safe mode:

- Choose > Restart.

  Your Mac restarts normally.

Starting in Verbose Mode

Starting your Mac in **verbose mode** displays a Terminal-like interface that lists scrolling technical messages during startup, including any startup errors. You may need the help of an IT professional or system administrator to interpret some of these status messages.

To start in verbose mode:

1 Shut down your Mac (> Shut Down).

2 Press and release the power button .

3 Immediately press and hold the Command+V keys (Figure 5.2).

4 Release the keys when scrolling text messages appear, meaning you've entered verbose mode.

5 Verbose mode exits automatically to the login window or desktop when the startup sequence completes. You can then use your Mac normally.

Command   V

Figure 5.2 Keyboard shortcut to start in verbose mode.

CHAPTER 6

Using OS X Recovery

OS X 10.7 (Lion) and later include **OS X Recovery**, a built-in set of tools that let you:

- Install or reinstall OS X (internet connection required)

- Restore OS X from a Time Machine backup

- Reset your password

- Check your internet connection or get help online by using Safari

- Verify and repair connected drives by using Disk Utility

Starting OS X Recovery

To start OS X Recovery:

1   Shut down your Mac (> Shut Down).

2   Press and release the power button Power .

3   Immediately press and hold the Command+R keys.

4   Release the keys when the Apple logo appears.

Tip: If you see a globe instead of the Apple logo, then the local recovery partition wasn't found or you're not connected to the internet.

---

5   After the startup sequence finishes, a desktop with an OS X Utilities window and menu bar appears.

Tip: If you see a login window or the normal desktop, then you probably didn't press and hold Command+R quickly enough. Restart your Mac and try again.

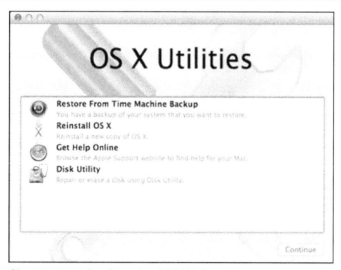

6   Choose an option from the OS X Utilities window or menu bar.

Resetting a Forgotten Password

You can use the Reset Password utility to reset a user's (or your own) password without administrative access.

Tip: This method won't work if FileVault encryption is turned on. Encrypted data are lost permanently if you forget the password. For details about FileVault, read the Apple support article "OS X: About FileVault 2" at *support.apple.com/ht4790*.

To reset a password:

1   Start OS X Recovery.

2   On the menu bar, choose Utilities > Terminal.

3   At the Terminal prompt, type resetpassword (one word) and then press Return.

    The Reset Password window opens, where you can reset a specific user's password.

4   When you're finished, restart your Mac (⌘ > Restart).

Tip: At the bottom of the Reset Password window is an ACL (Access Control List) utility that you can use to fix permissions for a specific user (Chapter 11).

Reinstalling OS X by Using the Recovery Partition

When you first install OS X, the installer silently creates a new partition on your hard drive that you can use to reinstall the operating system. (Your existing data are safely preserved during repartition.) This stealth partition, named Recovery HD, is invisible in Finder and Disk Utility, but you can see it by using the command `diskutil list` in Terminal. To recover OS X, hold down the Option key during startup and then choose Recovery HD when the list of startup partitions appears. You can also boot to Recovery HD from a locally connected Time Machine backup drive.

Tip: If FileVault encryption is turned on, Recovery HD won't appear when you hold down the Option key during startup, but you can still use OS X Recovery. For details about FileVault, read the Apple support article "OS X: About FileVault 2" at *support.apple.com/ht4790*.

CHAPTER 7

Network Settings and Diagnostics

You can use the Network panel of System Preferences (> System Preferences > Network) to inspect and troubleshoot your network and internet connections.

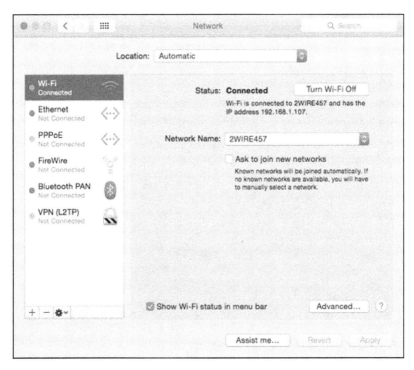

Connection Setup and Diagnostics

If you upgraded from an earlier version of OS X, your existing connections were preserved and should work fine. The network connection services list (on the left side of the Network panel) shows the ways that your computer is set up to connect to the internet or other network (a remote office or school network, for example): Ethernet (wired), Wi-Fi (wireless), External Modem (dial-up), Bluetooth, FireWire, VPN, and so on. A colored dot shows each connection's status: green means turned on and connected to a network; yellow means working, but not connected; and red means the connection isn't set up yet. Click any item in the list to view or change that connection's settings.

To set up a new connection:

- Click ⊞ , choose a connection type, and then configure the connection.

  or

  Click Assist Me > Assistant to set up a connection by stepping through a series of interview windows.

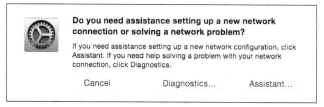

If you're having connection problems, start troubleshooting by running diagnostic tests: choose Assist Me > Diagnostics.

You can also troubleshoot by resetting network settings (Chapter 8) or configuring advanced settings (Chapter 9).

Connection Order

The order of connections in the services list is the sequence that OS X uses to go online when you open a browser or any program that needs internet or network access. OS X tries the first connection method; if that doesn't work, it tries the second, and so on. OS X can maintain multiple connections simultaneously—if a connection dies while you're using it, OS X switches automatically to the next. Laptop users usually sort the sequence by decreasing connection speed (or decreasing security): Ethernet, Wi-Fi, External Modem.

To set the order of connections:

1   Choose > System Preferences > Network.

2   Click [⚙▾] > Set Service Order.

3   Drag the items up and down in the services list into priority order.

CHAPTER 8

Resetting Network Settings

N etwork **locations** are intended for travelers who use different network settings in different places: Ethernet at work, wireless at home, dial-up when travelling, and so on. A "location" is actually a group of saved network settings that you can switch to easily.

Resetting All Network Settings

If you're unsure of what's causing a network problem, a quick and painless solution is to reset all your network settings by creating a new network location.

To reset network settings:

1   Choose > System Preferences > Network.

2   Choose Edit Locations from the Location pop-up menu (near the top of the panel).

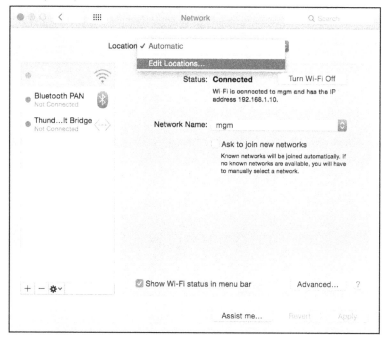

3 Click ➕, type a location name (such as *Test* or *Temp*), click Done, and then click Apply.

OS X silently resets your network settings in the background. If a yellow status indicator appears in the services list, then you haven't clicked Apply. A green indicator means that you probably can get back on the internet. If your connection still doesn't work, reset your modem or router (unplug it, wait 10 seconds, and then plug it back in).

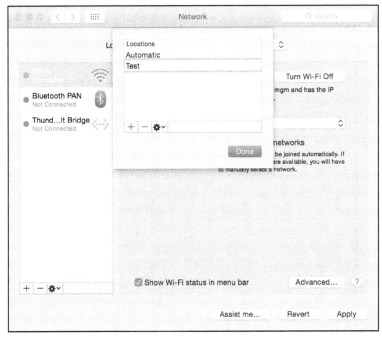

Tip: To switch to a location quickly (without opening Network preferences), choose > Location (this menu appears only after you set up more than one location).

Removing a Bad Network Location

After your network or internet connection is working properly, you can remove the bad network location.

To remove a bad network location:

1 Choose ■ > System Preferences > Network.

2 Choose Edit Locations from the Location pop-up menu (near the top of the panel).

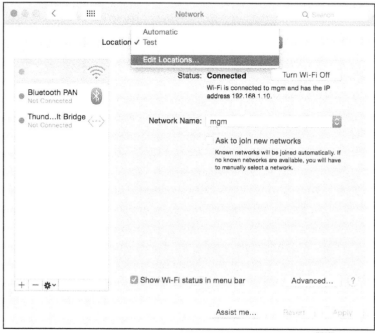

3 Select the bad location in the Locations list and then click ⊟.

The location is removed.

4 In the Locations list, select the good location that you created earlier (*Test* or *Temp* or whatever you named it).

5 Click ✿⁻ > Rename Location, type a new location name (such as *Automatic*, *Home*, or *Office*), click Done, and then click Apply.

CHAPTER 9

More Network Tricks

If your network or internet connection works but sometimes is slow or misbehaves, you can view or change the advanced network settings: choose > System Preferences > Network, click the Advanced button, and then click a tab (Wi-Fi, TCP/IP, and so on).

Controlling Wi-Fi Access

In the Wi-Fi pane, the Preferred Networks box lists the wi-fi networks that you've joined in the past. When wi-fi is turned on, your Mac will automatically join the first network in this list that's within range and available. If you've used your laptop at an airport recently, the public wi-fi network that you joined will be listed here. If you don't want to rejoin a particular network automatically, you can make your Mac "forget" it: select the target network in the list and then click ⊟ . To make your Mac instantly forget all wi-fi networks that you join, clear "Remember networks this computer has joined".

Tip: If multiple networks are available in the same location, you can drag networks up or down the list to reorder them. The available network that's highest in the list is joined first.

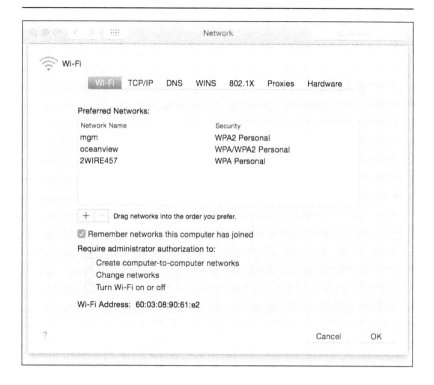

Diagnosing Wi-Fi Connection Problems

If you're having trouble loading webpages, sending or receiving email, or downloading or streaming music or video, then use the Wireless Diagnostics tool to try to diagnose wireless connectivity issues.

To use Wireless Diagnostics:

1 Hold down the Option key, click the 🛜 menu, and then click Open Wireless Diagnostics.

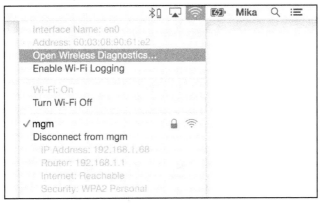

2 Click Continue to skip the introduction screen.

3 Type your user name and password when prompted. (You must be an administrator.)

The Wireless Diagnostics window opens. A progress bar appears while OS X checks your wi-fi settings and tests the wi-fi connection to your base station or router.

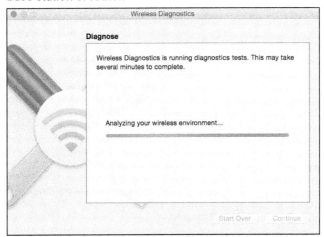

4 Follow the onscreen instructions.

Along the way, you can choose to monitor your wi-fi connection automatically for failures, enter information about your wireless network (such as your router make and model), or generate a summary diagnostics report.

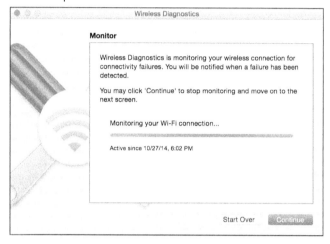

Tip: To see wireless network diagnostics quickly, hold down the Option key and click the 🛜 menu. Network diagnostics are shown in gray text under the name of the active network. The BSSID is the MAC (Media Access Control) address of the wireless access point. To see your Mac's MAC address (labeled "Wi-Fi Address"), choose > System Preferences > Network > Wi-Fi > Advanced > Wi-Fi pane. Some administrators secure networks by restricting access to only certain MAC addresses.

Renewing a DHCP Lease

If Wireless Diagnostics tells you that your internet connection is working as expected, but you still can't connect to the internet, try renewing your **DHCP (Dynamic Host Configuration Protocol)** lease: choose > System Preferences > Network > Advanced > TCP/IP tab > Renew DHCP Lease button. This command discards the current IP address and pulls a new IP address lease from the DHCP host (from your wireless router, for example), essentially reconnecting your computer to your router or modem.

Tip: Renewing a DHCP lease can also have a restorative effect when videos aren't playing properly or webpages are loading slowly.

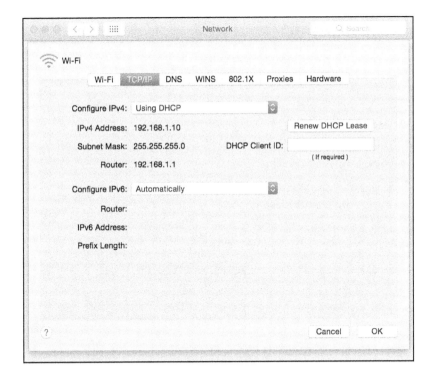

Changing the DNS Server

If your internet service provider (ISP) is having trouble with their **DNS** (domain name system) server, then you can substitute Google's DNS server address for your own to try to connect to the internet. Choose > System Preferences > Network > Advanced > DNS tab. Click (below the DNS Servers box), type *8.8.8.8*, and then click OK. Remember to switch back to your own DNS server later.

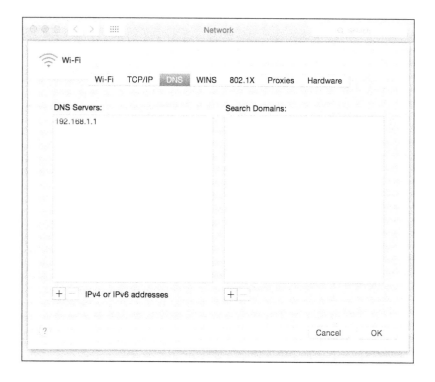

CHAPTER 10

Slow Computers

Symptoms of a slow computer include long load times, unresponsive applications, and the regular appearance of the spinning beach ball (also called the wait cursor). OS X provides tools that can help you resolve these issues.

Tip: To make sure that a spinning beach ball isn't the result of an unresponsive application, save your work and quit all applications. If you can't quit a particular application, choose > Force Quit, select the application, and then click Force Quit.

Updating Software

Running outdated software can adversely affect system or application performance. Apple regularly releases updates for OS X system software and other Apple programs. These updates include bug fixes, new features, security patches, version upgrades, and other improvements. All Apple software updates are available from the Updates section of the Mac App Store. Third-party programs downloaded from the App Store are also updated via the App Store.

Tip: If you didn't get a program from the App Store, check the developer's website for updates or use the program's built-in updater. To update Microsoft Office or Adobe Creative Cloud apps, for example, choose Help > Check for Updates. To update Mozilla Firefox or Google Chrome, choose Firefox > About Firefox or Chrome > About Google Chrome.

 By default, OS X automatically checks for updates every day, but you can check manually at any time. If any updates are available, App Store sends a notification and adds a numbered badge, denoting the number of updates, to the App Store's dock icon and menu entry.

To open App Store, choose > App Store. Available updates are listed in the Updates pane. To learn more about an update, click its icon or its *More* link. You can update any single item by clicking Update next to its name, or you can update everything by clicking Update All at the top of the window. You're also free to ignore updates.

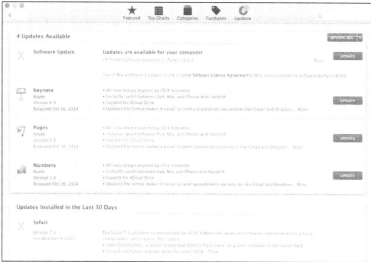

Tip: If you're on a large network, your network administrator might distribute updates via network server.

To set up software updates:

1 Choose > System Preferences > App Store.

2 Set the following options:

Automatically check for updates
Check for updates automatically and periodically.

Download newly available updates in the background
Download updates in the background without being asked. You'll still be notified before the updates are installed.

Install app updates
Install downloaded application updates without asking you.

Install OS X updates
Install downloaded OS X updates without asking you.

Install system data files and security updates
Install downloaded critical system updates without asking you.

Automatically download apps purchased on other Macs
Download apps (from the Mac App Store) that you bought on other Macs.

Show Updates
Open the Mac App Store and see any available updates.

Check Now
Check for updates manually.

Monitoring and Killing Processes

One of OS X's most useful tools for troubleshooting system slowdowns and other problems is Activity Monitor (Applications > Utilities > Activity Monitor). To open Activity Monitor quickly, press Command+Spacebar to open Spotlight search, type *activity monitor*, and then select Activity Monitor in the results list. You can use Activity Monitor to identify the programs and processes running on your computer, monitor their activity, and show statistics and graphs about CPU load, memory allocation, power consumption, drive activity, drive usage, and network traffic.

Tip: The Activity Monitor dock icon shows a real-time activity graph (View > Dock Icon).

In the following figure, the CPU pane of Activity Monitor shows that the first two processes (*Terminal* and *yes*) are consuming many CPU cycles relative to the other processes. If you select a process, you can inspect its details (View > Inspect Process or Command+I) or kill it (View > Quit Process or Option+Command+Q). Be careful not to kill a process unless you're certain that doing so won't cause system problems.

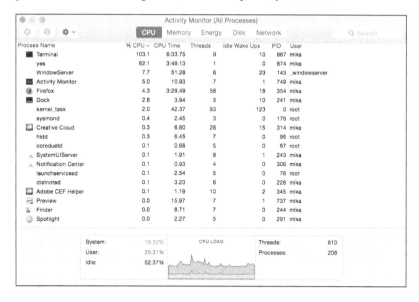

In the following figure, the Memory pane of Activity Monitor shows how much memory—physical (RAM) and virtual—is being allocated to apps and processes. The Memory Pressure graph at the bottom of the pane changes color (from green to yellow to red) to indicate increasing memory use. In this example, to free memory for other apps and processes, kill the first process (*Terminal*), provided that its death won't interfere with other processes.

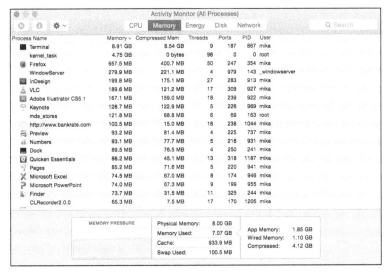

In the following figure, the Energy pane of Activity Monitor shows that the Terminal and FaceTime applications are hogging a lot of power. To preserve battery life, quit those apps.

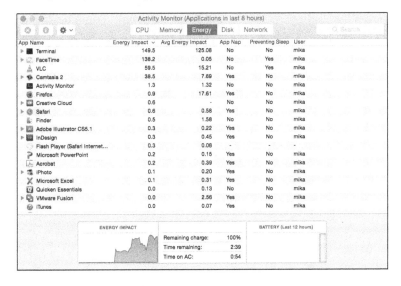

Freeing Storage Space

Freeing storage space has benefits beyond decluttering your drive and reclaiming space for newer or larger files. Many OS X system processes need a certain amount of free space to work optimally, so an overfilled startup drive can slow your Mac. A rule of thumb is that the startup drive should have about 5%–10% of its space free. If you have a 256 GB startup drive, for example, keep about 20 GB free. If you have a large (>500 GB) startup drive, you needn't keep more than 50 GB free no matter what its size. Your goal is to have enough space available so that OS X can shuffle around data easily without taxing the system to scrounge for space.

Tip: The drive on which OS X is installed, called the **system drive** or **startup drive**, usually is in the desktop's upper-right corner and is labeled *Macintosh* or *Macintosh HD*. If this drive icon isn't on your desktop, switch to Finder and then choose Go > Computer (Shift+Command+C) to see a list of available drives.

`39.6 GB available`   The easiest way to check remaining free space is to glance at the status bar at the bottom of any Finder window that's showing a folder on the startup drive (such as your Documents or Downloads folder). To show the status bar, in Finder, choose View > Show Status Bar (Command+/).

For a detailed look at how drive space is occupied, choose > About This Mac > Storage tab.

The main tool for performing drive-related tasks is Disk Utility (Applications > Utilities > Disk Utility). To open Disk Utility quickly, press Command+Spacebar to open Spotlight search, type *disk utility*, and then select Disk Utility in the results list.

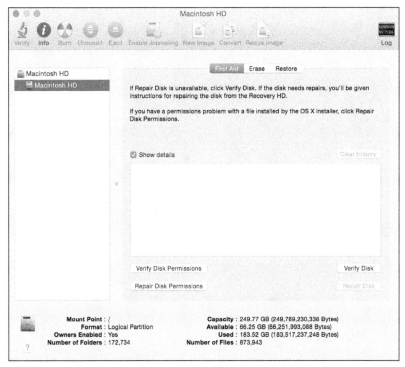

To check the health of the startup drive, select it in the drive list (on the left), click the First Aid tab, and then click the Verify Disk button. Disk Utility scans the drive to verify its integrity (formatting, read/write operations, and so on). If Verify Disk finds a problem, click the Repair Disk button.

If the startup drive is selected in Disk Utility, the Repair Disk button will be unavailable (dimmed) because you can't repair the drive that's currently running OS X. Instead, you must repair the startup drive by using Disk Utility within OS X Recovery (Chapter 6). You might want to first run Repair Disk Permissions (Chapter 11) to try to fix your problem, which *can* run on the current startup drive.

You shouldn't use your Mac while Verify Disk or Repair Disk is running, but if you do, your computer will probably run sluggishly until the process completes. After it completes, restart your Mac (> Restart).

Tip: The command-line interface for Disk Utility is the command `diskutil` in Terminal.

Permissions Problems

O S X's file system, like all file systems, has methods to assign **permissions** (access rights) to specific users and groups of users. The permissions system controls the ability of the users to view or make changes to the contents (files, settings, programs, and so on) of the file system.

Repairing Disk Permissions

Over time, as you install and remove programs from various sources, disk permissions change unintentionally, grow stale, and otherwise degrade. You can use Disk Utility (Applications > Utilities > Disk Utility) to repair disk permissions, which can be helpful if you're missing data or your Mac's performance has degraded (especially after a sudden power cut). You can also repair disk permissions as part of a general periodic maintenance plan.

To open Disk Utility, press Command+Spacebar to open Spotlight search, type *disk utility*, and then select Disk Utility in the results list. To repair disk permissions, select a drive in the drive list (on the left), click the First Aid tab, and then click the Repair Disk Permissions button.

You shouldn't use your Mac while Repair Disk Permissions is running, but if you do, your computer will probably run sluggishly until the process completes. After it completes, restart your Mac (⌘ > Restart).

Tip: The command-line interface for Disk Utility is the command `diskutil` in Terminal.

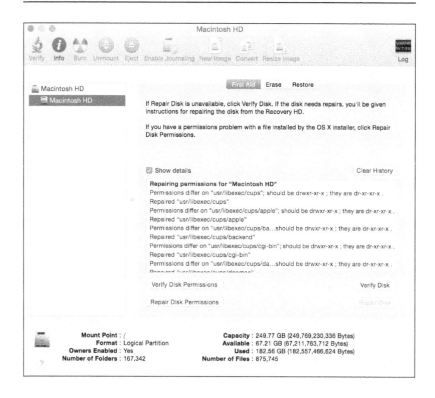

Changing File Permissions

A problem with file permissions can stop you from opening or editing a file. In the following example, the user lacks the permission to open the file named *Test.rtf*.

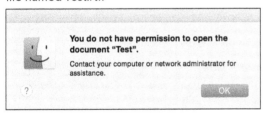

To change permissions for a file:

1   Select the file in Finder and then choose File > Get Info (Command+I), or right-click the file and then choose Get Info.

   The file's Info window opens. At the bottom of this window, the Sharing & Permissions box lists users and groups along with their permissions for this file. Here, the problem is that "everyone" has "No Access" to this file.

2 Click 🔒 and then type your user name and password when prompted. (You must be an administrator.)

3 Click ➕ (below the Sharing & Permissions box).

A window opens listing the user accounts that are available on your system.

4 Select a user or group name and then click Select.

The Sharing & Permissions box now lists the selected name and its default permission (here, "mika" has "Read only" access to the file).

5 Click the drop-down menu in the Privilege column for the user or group, and then choose the desired permission ("No Access", "Read only", or "Read & Write").

6 Close the Info window.

Tip: If you're comfortable with Unix, you can use the command **chmod** in Terminal to modify file permissions. The command **chmod 644 Test.rtf**, for example, makes the file *Test.rtf* readable by anyone and writable by only the file's owner. To learn how to use **chmod**, read the command's manual page by typing **man chmod**. (To learn how to use **man**, type **man man**.) A good number of books, guides, and webpages are devoted to teaching Unix for OS X.

CHAPTER 12

Errant System Preferences

System Preferences (> System Preferences) contains hundreds of settings that let you customize OS X. Some settings can cause problems if you activate them accidently or naively without knowing their full effects.

Here are some example preference to check:

Accessibility

The Accessibility panel—intended for disabled users with poor eyesight, hearing, or mobility—can be a source of much unexpected weirdness, owing to its many features that can be activated with accidental keyboard shortcuts. Rummage through Accessibility if your keyboard misbehaves (Keyboard), the mouse pointer jumps around (Mouse & Trackpad), your Mac reads onscreen items aloud (VoiceOver), strange color schemes appear (Display), or all or part of the screen suddenly enlarges (Zoom).

Bluetooth

If you're having a wireless connection problem with a particular Bluetooth device (mouse, wireless keyboard, printer, speakers, or whatever), turn the device off and then back on. If that doesn't work, use the Bluetooth panel to turn Bluetooth off and then back on. If that doesn't work, remove the device from the Bluetooth panel (click × next to its name in the Devices box) and then pair it again with your Mac.

Java

If you try to run an application and get a Java error, open the Java panel and update your version of Java.

Printers & Scanners

If you're having trouble printing, turn the printer off and then back on. If that doesn't work, delete and then reinstall the printer: select the printer in the Printers list, click ⎯ , and then disconnect and reconnect the printer to your Mac.

CHAPTER 13

Exploring OS X's Libraries

The various Library folders contain files used by OS X and your applications, including plug-ins, language dictionaries for the spell checker, Apple Help files, fonts, user preferences, printer drivers, and much more. These folders are often referenced in Apple support articles, online forums, troubleshooting guides, and Mac articles.

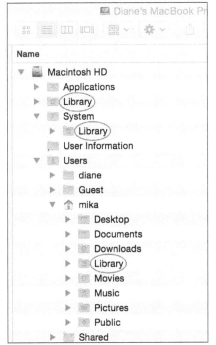

The Library folders are:

/System/Library
Don't change this folder.

/Library
This root-level folder stores items that are available to all users on your Mac. If everybody is having the same problem, check this folder. To open this folder, in Finder, choose Go > Computer (Shift+Command+C), open the OS X startup drive (typically named *Macintosh* or *Macintosh HD*), and then open the Library folder. In here you'll find folders contain shared items, including fonts, desktop backgrounds, and application plug-ins.

/Users/*user_name*/Library (or ~/Library)
Each user's home folder contains a personal Library folder, which contains many of the same types of files found in /Library, but available to only that user. To open this folder, in Finder, hold down the Option key and then choose Go > Library.

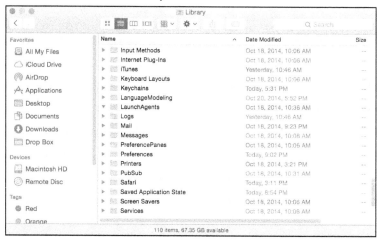

The two folders in ~/Library that you'll use most often are Preferences and Application Support:

- The Preferences folder contains many **.plist files** (property list files). Sometimes deleting an application's .plist file will fix a problem for that app. If you're having an issue with Safari, for example, remove the file *com.apple.Safari.plist* and then relaunch Safari.

- The Application Support folder contains app-specific data and support files. Each application is responsible for creating these directories as needed. If you have Firefox installed, for example, you'll see a Firefox folder here. The personal preferences that you set in Firefox—such as your home page, toolbar options, bookmarks, and saved passwords—are stored in the folder named Profiles in the Firefox folder.

Tip: If you're not sure whether deleting a file will fix a problem, move the file to your desktop rather than to the Trash, so that you can recover it easily if needed.

CHAPTER 14

Finding Solutions on the Web

No operating system provides a trouble-free experience. If you're struggling with strange bugs and problems that are beyond the scope of this book, then the best places to look for help are official Apple forums (*discussions. apple.com/welcome*), unofficial message boards, technical websites, and sites dedicated to Apple products and software. To get you started, here are some posts for OS X Yosemite-related bugs. Proceed at your own risk with esoteric or complex fixes.

- **Bluetooth.** The iDigitalTimes article *idigitaltimes.com/os-x-yosemite-problems-how-fix-wi-fi-bluetooth-connectivity-battery-life-safari-slow-mail-and-more* offers fixes for Bluetooth connectivity. The Apple forums thread *discussions.apple.com/thread/6608025* suggests that you reset NVRAM (PRAM) once or twice.

- **General problems.** See the MacRumors thread *forums.macrumors. com/showthread.php?t=1740402*, the Lifehacker article *lifehacker. com/how-to-fix-os-x-yosemites-biggest-annoyances-1646746016*, and the GottaBeMobile article *gottabemobile.com/2014/10/28/how-to-improve-os-x-yosemite-performance*.

- **Graphics.** See the (long) Apple forums thread *discussions.apple.com/thread/4766577*.

- **Handoff.** See the Gizmodo article *gizmodo.com/how-to-get-handoff-to-actually-work-in-os-x-yosemite-1651489730*.

- **iTunes updates.** See the Reddit thread *reddit.com/r/apple/comments/2joxlh/os_x_yosemite_1010_bug_thread/cldqb43*.

- **Mail.** See the Apple forums thread *discussions.apple.com/thread/6604139.*

- **Notification Center.** See the MacRumors thread *forums.macrumors.com/showthread.php?t=1803815* (apparently sourced from AppleCare: *apple.com/support/products*).

- **Photoshop.** See the Photoshop.com thread *feedback.photoshop.com/photoshop_family/topics/photoshop-cc-on-yosemite-graphics-problem.*

- **Safari.** For Netflix display errors, see the Apple forums thread *discussions.apple.com/thread/6620835.* If Safari is running slowly, see the Apple forums thread *discussions.apple.com/message/26857349.*

- **Sleep.** See the Reddit thread *reddit.com/r/apple/comments/2joxlh/os_x_yosemite_1010_bug_thread/clduh23.*

- **Spotlight.** If Spotlight Suggestions isn't working, see the Apple article *apple.com/ios/feature-availability/#spotlight-suggestions-spotlight-suggestions* to make sure that you're in a country where this feature is supported. See also the Reddit thread *reddit.com/r/apple/comments/2joxlh/os_x_yosemite_1010_bug_thread/cldpzkh.*

- **Wi-fi.** The Reddit thread *reddit.com/r/apple/comments/2jwah7/psa_yosemite_wifi_issues_list_of_possible_fixes* covers some advanced wi-fi hacks. The OS X Daily article *osxdaily.com/2014/10/25/fix-wi-fi-problems-os-x-yosemite* offers a step-by-step approach (some useful comments follow the article).

Index